COLOSSIANS -
HOPE IN
DESPERATE
TIMES

Studies by Kevin Jones

A  Publication

Published on behalf of MET by

MOORLEYS
Print, Design & Publishing
info@moorleys.co.uk · www.moorleys.co.uk

Published by
'Methodist Evangelicals Together'.
Revd D K Jones, 101 Viewfield Crescent, Sedgley
West Midlands, UK   DY3 3UL
Tel: 44 (0)1902 664773

ISBN 978 0 86071 782 9

e-mail kevtherev34@hotmail.com

First Edition published in United Kingdom 2019.

CONTENTS

Methodist Evangelicals Together
**is the largest independent organization in British Methodism today, a
renewal movement uniting and representing evangelicals at every level
within our denomination.**

Our three core purposes are:

- **ADVOCATING:** Promoting and representing evangelicalism within Methodism, and Wesleyan evangelicalism within the wider evangelical world.
- **EQUIPPING:** Providing resources through publications, conferences and our website for evangelicals within British Methodism.
- **SUPPORTING:** Offering pastoral support and advice to evangelicals, who can often feel isolated within Methodism and face particular pressures.

MET is a fellowship for every Methodist who shares our desire to:

- Uphold the authority of Scripture
- Seek Spiritual Renewal
- Pray for Revival
- Spread Scriptural holiness
- Emphasise the centrality of the Cross

MET promotes partnership in the Gospel to proclaim Jesus as Lord. Our partners include:

- Cliff College
- ECG
- LWPT
- Share Jesus International
- Inspire Network

Join MET and partner with us to:

- *Network with evangelical Methodists in prayer and action.*
- *Add your voice to 1700 others on key issues at all levels of the Methodist Church and beyond.*
- *Participate in national and local events.*
- *Receive the MET Connexion Magazine.*

Find us at: www.methodistevangelicals.org.uk

or write to us
c/o Moorleys Print & Publishing, 23 Park Road, Ilkeston, Derbys DE7 5DA
who will pass on your valued enquiry.

COLOSSIANS INTRODUCTION

Paul's letter to Colosse, written from his Roman imprisonment around AD60, deals with a distortion of the gospel. The church was in danger of being deceived. Bad Christian practice always rises from bad Christian doctrine, and the best protection for Christian ethics is a sound understanding of the person and work of Christ. In brief, what we believe profoundly affects what we do.

The problem Paul addressed was a reliance on religious ritual, Jewish laws and personal experience, as the basis of the Christian faith. It was a Jewish/experience-based heresy and many of the elements of their error are re-emerging in the church today. Such teaching is called syncretism. It adds elements from the prevailing culture to the Christian faith and, by doing so, waters down the unchanging truth of the gospel until it is no gospel at all.

The gospel will always stand on the foundation of the Old Testament and spring from the New Testament teaching of the Apostles (Ephesians 2:20). Any teaching that denies the truth, unity, authority and inspiration of Scripture provides an excuse for error, both moral and theological. What was at stake was the very essence of the faith, the Divinity of Jesus Christ. Paul takes us to the heights of Divine revelation by showing that *'In Christ all the fullness of the Deity lives in bodily form'* (2:9).

Paul also shows that our salvation has two stages, a past work and a present work. We are saved through Christ's work on the cross, when we are united to Him by faith. It is through our union with Christ that His forgiveness is known. God in Christ has taken the written code of the law that stands against us and nailed it to the cross (2:4-15). Colossians defines the essence of the person and the work of Christ. It is a Christ-centred and Christ-exalting book. If we would know the depths and height of our faith, we too must understand the essence of the person and work of Christ.

This is not an exhaustive study guide, but is written for preachers, students and groups who want to go deeper into the heart of the Christian faith. As we study Colossians we will find it is both practical and relevant to today. The chapters provide an exposition of the Scriptures and, with the questions, a means to go deeper in group studies. Since good doctrine will always produce godly conduct, and bad doctrine will invariably produce a distorted version of the Christian faith, we must *'set our minds on things above, not on earthly things'* and *'put to death whatever belongs to our earthly nature: sexual immorality, impurity, lust, evil desires and greed, which is idolatry'. Because of these, the wrath of God is coming'* (3:1, 5-6). These were dangerous times; only a full understanding of Christ's person and purpose and God's call to personal holiness could save the church.

I trust you will enjoy this study of the majesty of Jesus and the message of salvation as revealed in the book of Colossians.
Rev D Kevin Jones, Sedgley, 2019.

Chapter One
KNOWING GOD
Colossians 1:1-14

Why write to the Colossians?

Paul's Greeting v1-2
(The Apostle – The Saints – grace, mercy and peace.)

Paul's Thanksgiving v3-8
(Truth – Faith – Love – Hope.)

Paul's Prayer v9-14
(Knowledge of God, qualified to serve, delivered from evil.)

Why did Paul write to the Colossians? He has never been to Colosse, so the question arises, who is he writing to and why is he writing?

Colosse was a Roman colony, a small market town, it was a little isolated and off the beaten track and mostly bypassed by travellers. It lay 100 miles inland from the famous sea port of Ephesus, in the Lycus valley, and 10 miles from the more famous Laodicea. Colosse had a fairly strong Jewish community who were forcibly deported there under Antiochus Epiphanies the Seleucid king 200 years earlier, when he sacked Jerusalem in 168BC, and became ruler of the eastern portion of Alexander the Great's Empire. This means that there was an immediate mission field for the message of Christ and some understanding of the promises of God among the Hebrew exiles. It also laid the new congregation open to the attack of Judaizers, Christians who believed that it was still necessary to keep the Old Testament religious rules on diet, festivals and ceremonies.

Paul had not founded this church; however, he stayed at Ephesus for almost 3 years, and Acts 19:10 tells us *'All the Jews and Greeks who lived in the province of Asia heard the word of the Lord.'* One of the people who heard the message of the Messiah was Epaphras, who has now arrived at Paul's door seeking his advice. Paul is under house arrest in Rome (Acts 28:30-31). It is here that he probably welcomes Epaphras.

He writes to the church, *'We have heard of your faith in Christ Jesus and of the love you have for all the saints - that you have already heard... the word of truth, the gospel... you learned it from **Epaphras, our dear fellow-servant**, who is a **faithful minister of Christ'*** (1:4-7).

It seems Epaphras is the 'minister' of the church and actually planted the church in his home town; it probably met in the home of Philemon. However, some false teachers have arrived to challenge Epaphras. He goes to Paul for advice and counsel. From his imprisonment, Paul writes to set out the true Gospel revealed in Jesus Christ. The problem was that this little church was being told they needed Christ plus something else. Jesus was a way to God but not the exclusive way to God. Faith in Jesus was a starting point but not the finishing line, and it sounds plausible. Christ PLUS was the teaching of the Judaizers, Christ plus secret knowledge, Christ plus Angelic mediators, Christ plus strict discipline and observance of rituals. (Asceticism)

The most important thing is to realise that Christ is all we need, we don't need Christ plus, we need more of Christ, we need a deeper and fuller understanding of and obedience to *'Christ, in whom are hidden all the treasures of wisdom and knowledge'* (2:2-3). We don't need new wisdom but we need to *'grow in the knowledge of God'* (1:10). We need the *'Word of Christ to dwell in us richly'* (3:16).

1:   PAUL'S GREETING 1:1-2

Paul introduces himself as an **Apostle**, by the **will of God**. The question is, who had appointed these other teachers? An Apostle is a 'sent one,' someone carrying the power and authority of the sender. You cannot volunteer to be an Apostle, Jesus Himself called Paul on the Road to Damascus, specifically to reach the Gentile nations (Acts 22:21).

Paul writes, to the Saints, in Greek the 'Haggios', holy and faithful brothers. What is a saint? Some extra holy person? No, all who have accepted the call to follow Christ are called saints. They have been called out of the world and into a relationship with God in Christ. They stand in a new relationship to **each other** as brothers and sisters, but God's name for His people is Saints.

His greeting is, '*Grace to you and peace from God our Father and the Lord Jesus Christ*' (1:2).

Grace and peace are important concepts in the Christian life. Grace is unearned favour, God's favour on us in spite of what we have done. God saves us as an act of grace, not because of anything we have done, but because He has determined in Himself to be gracious.

A difference between grace and mercy is that **'in His grace'** God gives us what we do not deserve - favour and sonship. **'In His mercy'** He does not give us the punishment we do deserve. Mercy is forgiveness offered, grace is blessing bestowed. It is what the father offered the prodigal son when he returned, expecting to be a servant. Instead he received the ring of sonship, the cloak of righteousness, the shoes of dignity and the feast of a lifetime (Luke 15:21-25). This is grace.

Peace: Receiving God's grace brings us into a new relationship of peace with God, who is now our Father, and with Jesus Christ who is now our Lord.

2:   PAUL'S THANKSGIVING 1:3-8

These people at Colosse are beginning to follow a dangerous error. How does Paul treat them? In Galatia, one of his own churches, he wrote, *'You foolish Galatians! Who has bewitched you?'* (Galatians 3:1).

Here, he is not heavy handed. He instructs and teaches them; instead of pointing out their foolishness he proclaims the supremacy of Christ. In effect he says 'put Christ first and all these things will follow.' Jesus said the same in Matthew 6:33.

i: He supports Epaphras.
ii: He sets out the official apostolic teaching.
iii: He shows that true teaching will lead to a holy life and error will lead to immorality.
iv: He shows that the Gospel is the same over all the world.

Next, he gives thanks that they have accepted the truth. He is not thanking them that they have accepted 'the **word of truth**,' the gospel. He is thanking **God** for their salvation – they have heard and received the truth of God in Christ. John describes the process by which people are saved in John 5:24, *'whoever **hears my word** and **believes** Him who sent me **has eternal life** and will not be condemned; he has **crossed over from death** to life.'* First, we hear the word; once we hear, we make a conscious decision to believe in both the message and the messenger. As we believe, we are given the gift of eternal life. Hearing alone is not enough, we must hear <u>and</u> believe in order to receive eternal life. When we do, there is a change in our status, we cross from death to life.

For Christians truth is very important. Jesus said, *'I am the way, the truth, and the life'* (John 14:6 NKJV). Some people will accept truths, but not one ultimate truth. For them there are many truths, and each one is as valid as the other, even when one supposed truth contradicts another it does not seem to matter. For us truth is embodied in a person, and that person brings the truth of the Gospel.

The Gospel is true. The word Gospel means Good News, we preach and teach the good news of the truth of Jesus Christ, God with us, who died and rose again for our sin. The truth is that God will forgive all our sin and accept us into His family if we will place our full faith in Jesus. We do not need more than Jesus, it is not about what we have done, it is about what Christ has accomplished.

This truth should give us confidence but never arrogance. So that *'speaking the truth in love, may grow up in all things into Him who is the head — Christ'* (Ephesians 4:15 NKJV).

Truth should affect our attitude.

The three Christian attitudes shown here **are Faith, Love and Hope**.

Our faith is in Christ. This is important since these people are beginning to think they need more than Christ. Faith is the **first step**, in the Christian walk. *'For by grace you have been saved through faith, and that not of yourselves; it is the gift of God, not of works, lest anyone should boast'* (Ephesians 2:8-9 NKJ).

Faith is not only the door it is also the road we walk on, faith is not passive but active and inquiring. We can build up our faith, as we seek to receive God's word and apply it to our lives. *'Faith comes by hearing, and hearing by the word of God'* (Romans 10:17-18 NKJV).

Faith prompts love, not just love of God, but love of God's people. A sure sign that someone has faith is that they begin to love the people of God, 'warts' and all. We may be saints, but we still test each other's faith. The Colossians passed this test, *'we have heard... about your love for all the Saints'* (1:4) says Paul. Love is active, it must show itself. It is no use saying you love people if you never show it, because if you don't show love you don't really love. Love is a passion and a desire that must be expressed and love is never selfish. If it is selfish it is not love. Love is the selfless giving of one's time, talents and devotion to another, not because they deserve it but because you have determined in your heart to love.

The third virtue is Hope. Christian hope is not a 'hope so' attitude, the vague optimism that things will get better in time. The Christian's hope is a confidence in the promises of God. Its main focus is not God's provision on earth, but His reward in heaven. There is a *'Hope which **is laid up** for you in heaven'* (1:5), like a treasure stored safely for our arrival. Their hope in God's promises actually prompted their faith and love. For the Colossians, a future hope beyond this life, was the bedrock of their faith, *'the faith and love **that spring from the hope** that is stored up for you in heaven'* (1:5 NIV).

Our future hope is supposed to affect our lives today. Children know this. Birthday, Christmas, holiday are all exciting things to look forward to. Business knows this, they set a vision and a goal in order to reap a future profit. Have Christians forgotten that our hope is stored in heaven, not in this life? The ideas of being inspired by a vision actually comes from the Christian faith. Paul closed his thanksgiving by commending Epaphras, *'our **dear fellow servant**, who is **a faithful minister of Christ*** *on your behalf, who also **declared to us your love** in the Spirit'* (1:7-8 NKJV).

Paul gives him high praise. Epaphras is a fellow servant who is precious to Paul and a faithful minister, he has proved himself over time and can be trusted. Above all this, Paul recognises the authentic work of the Holy Spirit being described by Epaphras. Today it is hard to recognise the voice of the Holy Spirit from the voices of people. The keys are the truth of the Gospel and the exaltation of Christ. What Christ is as the living word, He has also revealed in the written word; therefore, the Holy Spirit will never lead us to do anything contrary to the truth of God's word. Nor will the Holy Spirit lead us to place Christ in second place. The Colossians have the Spirit, now they must hold on to the truth and not be deceived.

3:   PAUL'S PRAYER 1:9-14

Here he begins to show the supremacy of Christ. Paul borrows some of the words the false teachers use, but reveals their true meaning. The false teachers were interested in secret **knowledge,** which would **qualify** them to know God better, and **deliver** them from the evil of this world.

Knowledge is not an end in itself, it must lead to obedience of God's will: *'We have not stopped praying for you and asking God to fill you with the **knowledge of His will** through all spiritual wisdom and understanding'* (1:9).

The false teachers taught that knowledge was the means to salvation. Jehovah's Witnesses and Mormons do the same today. They believe they alone have the secret knowledge that leads to salvation. We are not saved by knowledge; we are saved by faith in Christ. Secret knowledge that is only for the initiate is attractive, it is the hook the Freemasons use to draw people in. The false teachers promise knowledge about the nature of the universe, about good and evil, about humanity and about God. [These Judaizers were following the early Gnostic teachings.] We still use the term gnostic in our word, agnostic, describing someone who does not know. These were those who believed they were in the know, and that their secret knowledge would lead to salvation. The pursuit of knowledge rather than the pursuit of faith has been the ancient temptation for all believers (See Genesis 3). Understanding more of God should lead to a deeper love and a deeper humility. Following knowledge as the means of salvation only leads to divisions and pride.

A sure sign of a false religion is that it is not for all, but it is only for the initiated. In contrast Paul shows the universal application of the gospel, *'All over the world* this gospel is bearing fruit and growing' (1:6). God's message is to all, there is no private message for the Colossian church, they were susceptible because they were geographically isolated; small churches who are isolated can face the same danger today.

God wants to guide His people to 'the knowledge of his will,' through, 'spiritual wisdom and understanding' (1:9). God's wisdom is always meant to lead us to live a holy life. God's will, revealed by the Holy Spirit to the human spirit, is 'spiritual,' moral and practical. He writes to the Colossians, praying that they 'may **live a life worthy of the Lord**' (1:10). God is willing to guide us but we can miss His guidance if we do not pray.

True teaching and Holy living are always linked, 'so that you will **walk in a manner worthy** of the Lord, to please Him in all respects, bearing fruit in every good work' (1:10 NASU).

The purpose of our life is not the acquisition of knowledge but to learn to walk with God. The term 'walk' takes us back to the Garden of Eden where Adam walked with God and God walked with Adam (Genesis 3:8).

Wrong teaching will always lead to wrong living, false doctrine prompts faithless actions. True teaching leads to a life that is pleasing to the Lord. Holiness is not a matter of choice it is a matter of obedience.

The false teaching was that the created world was evil. This meant that God could not become flesh; since He could not associate with what was evil. This false teaching did not exalt Christ but relegated Him to being either just another human prophet, or no more than one of many mediators between God and humanity. Since they taught that God could not be part of an evil creation, they believed that He sent out emanations, levels of beings, angels and demons as intermediaries between us and God. We could not know God directly but must deal with these Angelic beings. We find almost the same teaching today in new age books with titles like 'how to recognise your Guardian angel' or 'your angel, your guide'. People are seeking angels as if they were somehow separated from God and were more important than God.

This teaching denied God's word as revealed by the Apostles. Paul is adamant that Christ was indeed God and took on human flesh. *'For in Christ all the fullness of the Deity lives in bodily form'* (2:9). It is true that the world is fallen, but it is not true that God has no ability to interact with the world, or that we have to come through intermediaries. *'For there is one God and one mediator between God and human being, the man Christ Jesus'* (1Timothy 2:5). In Colossians, Paul deals with the Deity of Christ; He is God with us. His Christology is some of the highest in the New Testament.

There are three things that the church must never forget. The deity of Christ, His substitutionary atoning death and that the saved are called to holiness. When we step away from these, we are following another Gospel, which is no longer based on truth.

Next, we find that wrong teaching leads to a wrong attitude, that the body is evil therefore you must bring it into submission by ascetic practices such as fasting, ceremonies and observing religious days and festivals (2:16, 20-23).

What we believe affects how we live. The Colossians did not need special spiritual ceremonies, they were to show their faith by the way they lived their lives, in *'patience and long suffering with joy'* (1:11 NKJV). Usually we need to be patient through difficult situations and long-suffering with people. Joy is the gift of God that sustains us in our trials, *'the joy of the LORD is your strength'* (Nehemiah 8:10). In all these things God walks with us and His presence makes the feast.

Qualified: The false teachers believed these Angelic powers could keep us from or bring us into God's kingdom. Without their teaching we could never qualify for the favour of God. The problem with pursuing knowledge is that there is always one more thing to know, one more thing before we qualify. It is an endless tyranny. I almost fell into this trap in my 40's. I had followed Christ for many years and now had two degrees in Theology. In most places that I went to, I knew more about God than anyone else in the room. However, I came to realise that though I knew about God, I did not really know Him closely anymore. There was an inner aching for an experiential knowledge of God, rather than an academic one. At that point I began a search for the presence of God. Seeking His face and not His hand, has drawn me closer to His heart, and wonderfully continues to this day. Knowledge about God provides a foundation but is not the answer to knowing God. We are qualified to know Him through the finished work of Christ, we must now learn to enter into His most Holy Presence, in heart-felt worship.

As Paul reveals to the Colossians, *'giving thanks to the Father, who **has qualified** you to share in the inheritance of the saints in the kingdom of light'* (1:12). If God says you qualify, then you qualify. The only question is: do you draw near? This takes us back to grace since it is 'only by grace can we enter.' There may be a hint at rituals done in the dark, but God brings everything into the light. God's secrets are open secrets, because all who seek Him will find Him (Luke 11:9-13).

You already share in the inheritance of the saints. In the Old Testament the inheritance was land, in the New Testament the inheritance is sonship, and a down payment of the kingdom to come in the ministry and presence of the Holy Spirit (Ephesians 1:13-14).

Delivered: To be delivered, rescued or translated, made sense to this community because of Antiochus. He transferred a whole population from Israel to Colosse and as a victor planted them there. Christ our deliverer has also conquered and removed a people from the kingdom of darkness. He has translated/removed and delivered His people into the kingdom of light. In Exodus, the deliverance was out of Egypt. Our deliverance is into a new kingdom, the kingdom of the Son He loves.

The cost of this deliverance was His blood and the debt it paid was the list of our sins (2:14-15). Paul is telling them that they have all they need in Christ. He is the beloved Son *'in whom we have redemption'* (1:13-14). If God loves Christ and we are in Him, then how does God feel about us? The answer is that He also loves us. We qualify for deliverance through Christ.

Paul greets the church as an Apostle of grace to the saints in Colosse.

He is thankful that by the ministry of Epaphras, God has saved them, producing faith, love and hope in their lives.

His prayer is that they may grow in the true knowledge of God, being guided in His will and in holiness of life. They should not worry that they are second class, because they qualify for all that God has in Christ, who has delivered them by His blood.

Questions for Groups
Colossians 1:1-14

Please take the Bible and read the chapter out loud before answering the questions.

Verses 1-2

1.   If you were introducing yourself to people who had never met you, how would you describe yourself?
2.   What is significant about Paul's introduction?
3.   How does Paul address the Colossians? Why?
4.   The error at Colosse was seeing Christ as one among many. How does Paul refute this and where is this attitude found today?

Verses 3-8

5.   Why did Paul write this letter?
6.   What does Paul give thanks for?
7.   What are the three characteristics of a believer?
8.   What does Paul mean by the Word of Truth?

Verses 9-14

9.   What do we pray about the most?
10.   What did Paul pray for the Colossians?
11.   How can we know God's will?
12.   What attitude pleases God?
13.   What does good theology produce?
14.   What does bad theology produce?
15.   If Christ is the Son of God's love and we are in Christ, how does he feel about us?

To close your study, ask: Are there any practical things I need to do as a result of looking at the introduction?

Then pray around the issues your group has covered.

Chapter Two
THE SUPREMACY OF CHRIST
Colossians 1:15-23

His Supreme Person v15
(The image of the invisible.)

His Supreme Status v15-17
(First born - Creator - before - holding together.)

His Supreme Mission v19-22
(Reconciliation.)

His Supreme Purpose v22-23
(Holiness.)

Have you ever listened to someone enthusiastically telling you about what they believe, only to find out half way through that you don't agree, but you can't really say why? This is where Epaphras is. He is the pastor of this Church and false teachers have infiltrated the congregation. He needs the guidance of the Apostle Paul. This is what false teaching sometimes does; it causes us to think more deeply about what we really believe. False teaching can help us to express the truth more clearly, as we begin to wrestle with what we really believe.

The false teachers were proclaiming that they had a hidden knowledge. They did not resist faith in Christ, they relegated faith in Christ to second place. They said that believing in Christ was the beginning of the walk, but that there were more significant powers than Christ. They believed in Christ plus angels, Christ plus circumcision, Christ plus observing Jewish ceremonies. Paul sets out the teaching clearly that it is not Christ plus, it is Christ alone.

## 1:	HIS SUPREME PERSON *'the image of the invisible God'* (1:15)

Many people's image of Jesus is of the baby in the manger at Bethlehem or teaching and doing miracles, feeding 5000 people, walking on water, but Paul introduces Him as supreme over the universe.

Jesus is described as, *'the image of the invisible God'* (1:15). Images have two functions, they **depict and they disclose**, an image reveals what the one depicted is like. Once you see an accurate image you understand something more of the thing or person that is represented.

Now, in the Old Testament the making of images is strictly forbidden: *'You shall not make for yourself a carved image, or any likeness of anything that is in heaven above, or that is in the earth beneath, or that is in the water under the earth; you shall not bow down to them nor serve them. For I, the LORD your God, am a jealous God'* (Exodus 20:4-5). The problem with an image of God is that it debases God. If you represent His strength, you cannot represent His compassion, if you represent His love you cannot represent His judgement. An image cannot represent or disclose anything about the majesty of God. God is Spirit and no man-made representation can capture His majesty.

We have a problem with knowing what God is like because He is invisible. If we want to know what God is like we have no frame of reference.... until Paul tells us that Christ is the *'image of the invisible God.'* If you want to know what God is like, look to Jesus. *'God was pleased to have all his fullness dwell in him'* (1:19). Jesus not only **depicts** God to us, he **reveals** God to us. Jesus is the invisible God, made visible.

Only in Jesus is the full majesty of God adequately made known. Jesus is the die-cast image of God.

2:   HIS SUPREME STATUS. The *'FIRST BORN'*

This term causes problems for some; they assume that first born, means born or created first, thus denying both Christ's Divinity and eternity. The title *FIRST BORN* is not always about chronology, it is ALSO about pre-eminence. Biblically, the firstborn in a family has the right of **inheritance**, they inherit the family farm, name and blessing, they hold the chief status in the family.

How would you finish this list of descendants, Abraham, Isaac and _ _ _ _ _? The truth is that Jacob was not the first born, but because Esau despised his birth-right and did not think his primacy was important, Jacob supplanted him.

In the same way Solomon was not David's first-born son but he has the status of the first born when he becomes King. *'I will also appoint him my firstborn, the most exalted of the kings of the earth. I will maintain my love to him for ever, and my covenant with him will never fail. I will establish his line for ever, his throne as long as the heavens endure'* (Psalm 89:27-29).

Jesus and the title 'FIRST BORN': The term 'first born' is used of Jesus many times in the Bible. In the Christmas story, where Christ steps into time and takes on human flesh, 'first born' is chronological and literally means born first. He was the first child that Mary had. [She had other children see Matthew 12:26, Mark 3:31-32, Luke 8:19-21, John, 2v12, Acts 1:14.] *'She brought forth her firstborn Son, and wrapped Him in swaddling cloths, and laid Him in a manger, because there was no room for them in the inn'* (Luke 2:7 NKJV). Also, when He is resurrected from the dead, He is called *'the firstborn from among the dead'* (1:18). Only at His birth into this world and His resurrection out of this world is there a chronological meaning to the term 'first born'.

In the letter to the Romans, Jesus is called *'**the firstborn among many brothers**'* (Romans 8:29). He is the head of the family, the chief among all believers. He was the first to bear the likeness of God, among men, He is the elder brother with the rights of inheritance, but He is not the last, to bear God's image - through Christ we too bear the likeness of God in our soul, we are the many brothers.

In **Hebrews** 12:23 the church is called *'the church **of the firstborn**, whose names are written in heaven.'* That means He has supremacy over and ownership of the church. The church is His inheritance. 1:18 calls Christ the *'head of the body, the church.'* This is not a building; He is head of the people of God. 1:19 has *'First born from the dead.'*

Here in Colossians He is called *'the firstborn over all creation'* (1:15-16), first in status and first in authority, He is the one who has the right to rule over creation. He is not created, He is uncreated and existed before creation began.

Why should Christ rule creation? The answer is that He made it, *'by him all things were created'* (1:16). **I thought God created** the world, and that is true. Who created a building the designer or the builder? They both did. The picture we are given here is that God was the designer, Jesus was the master builder. He is there at the beginning of creation, it was made *by Him* and He owns creation, it is created *for Him*. At the end of time creation itself will be Christ's inheritance, given to Him by the Father.

In the meantime, He is still looking after his creation, *'He is before all things and in him all things hold together'* (1:17). 'Before' means He is pre-eminent and pre-existent. He existed before and is supreme over His creation.

False teachers taught that knowledge was the means to salvation. Jehovah's witnesses and Mormons follow the same route today. We are not saved by knowledge; we are saved by faith in Christ. Secret knowledge for the initiate is attractive, like the Freemasons today. The false teachers promised knowledge about the nature of the universe, about good and evil, about humanity and about God. These early Gnostics claimed special knowledge.

The actual false teaching was that the created world was evil. This meant that God could not become flesh since He could not associate with what was evil. Therefore, God has sent out emanations, levels of beings, angels and demons between us and God, we could not know God directly but must deal with these Angelic beings. We find almost the same teaching today in the new age books with titles like 'how to recognise your Guardian angel', 'your angel, your guide'. People are seeking angels as if they were somehow separated from God and were more important than God.

The Gnostics used three words to define their teaching, **Knowledge, qualified, delivered.** Paul borrows the words and prays for *'God to fill you with the knowledge of His will through all spiritual wisdom and understanding'* (1:1). We are to give *'thanks to the Father, who has qualified you to share in the inheritance of the saints in the kingdom of light'* (1:12), *'He has delivered us from the power of darkness and conveyed us into the kingdom of the Son of His love'* (1:13). All we need is already accomplished in Christ, we do not need other mediators. We need more of Jesus.

Wrong teaching leads to a wrong attitude, that the body is evil therefore you must bring it into submission by ascetic practices, and wrong attitudes lead to wrong actions, such as fasting, ceremonies and observing religious days and festivals (ch2). What we believe affects how we live.

The Colossians did not need special spiritual ceremonies. Then Paul says, almost as a throw-away comment, Jesus also created the angelic beings, calling them *'dominions, principalities or powers'* (1:16 NKJV).

1:16 has 3 prepositions **by, through and for**. *'For **by** Him all things were created, both in the heavens and on earth, visible and invisible, whether thrones or dominions or rulers or authorities — all things have been created **through** Him and **for** Him'* (NASB). The picture we are given is of Christ as first born, king of creation; His is the originator and ruler of all that is.

3:   HIS SUPREME MISSION: 'Reconciliation.'

'God was pleased… to reconcile to Himself all things, by making peace through His blood shed on the cross' (1:19-20). He came to *reconcile* us to God by *His blood*. The old way did not work.

Someone may ask why we need reconciling to God. The answer is that because of our spiritual and psychological standing we are enemies of God. Both our thought patterns and our way of life are an offence to the Holy God. *'Once you were alienated from God and were enemies in your minds because of your evil behaviour'* (1:21). We don't see ourselves as enemies. We think we are good people, we make mistakes but we don't see ourselves as enemies of God. Until we are reconciled it is very difficult for us even to see our need.

The greatest need of humanity is forgiveness of sin.

> 'If   our <u>greatest</u> need   had   been   information, God <u>would</u> have sent an educator.
>
> If   our <u>greatest</u> need   had   been   technology, God <u>would</u> have sent us a scientist.
>
> If our <u>greatest</u> need had been money, God <u>would</u> have sent us an economist. But <u>since</u> our <u>greatest</u> need was forgiveness,
>
> God sent us a Saviour.' **Max Lucado**

Because we could not reconcile ourselves, God Himself has acted to reconcile us, and reconciliation is hard work. In South Africa the commission on reconciliation worked for years to bring about and preserve the peace. Israel and Palestine, seem implacably opposed, there is no one to reconcile the differences. If we are to be reconciled, someone has to settle the differences of the two sides.

Forgiveness is the Key, God has gone to extraordinary lengths, *'God was pleased to have all His fulness dwell in Him, and through Him to reconcile to Himself all things, whether things on earth or things in heaven, by making peace through his blood'* (1:19-20).

He makes peace, the two sides are at war. Paul uses strong words - alienated, accusation, blemish, enemies. *'But now He has <u>reconciled you</u> **by Christ's physical body through death**'* (1:22).

Accusations came from the law, we were condemned as those who broke the law of God, but the law's price has been paid and we can now be reconciled.

It is Christ's death that gives us life. We are forgiven and Jesus introduces us and presents us to the Father. *'Christ has* brought you into the very presence of God, and you are standing there before him with nothing left against you - nothing left that he could even chide you for' (1:22 TLB).

What are you going to do about it? There is still a battle for the mind, Christ did not die to make us wise, but to make us holy.

4:   HIS SUPREME PURPOSE: 'Holiness.'

To 'present you holy without blemish and free from accusation, if you continue in your faith established and firm, not moved from the hope held out in the gospel' (1:22-23).

Salvation has three parts: we **were** saved, we **are being saved** and we **will be saved**. The full price to reconcile us to God was paid on the cross, His blood was the cost, not religion or angels or special knowledge.

We must still do something, we must continue with Jesus. He will make us holy '*if we continue in our faith established and firm, not moved from the hope held out in the gospel*' (1:22-23).

Some believers at Colosse were obviously falling away. Faith is the Key, but real faith produces a determination to follow Jesus. We cannot save ourselves but we can make sure we continue in the faith. Perseverance is the response of the faithful heart.

The sign of a true faith is a **changed mind and a changed life**. Sometimes we must break with old friends and old ways.

Christians think differently from their work colleagues, families and friends, '*Do not conform any longer to the pattern of this world but be transformed by the renewing of your mind'* (Romans 12:2).

We have a new focus to our ideas, *'seek those things which are above, where Christ is, sitting at the right hand of God. Set your mind on things above, not on things on the earth'* (3:1-3 NKJV).

The false teachers preached salvation through secret knowledge. Paul explains the Secret or *'mystery -- hidden for generations, -- is Christ in you, the hope of glory'* (1:26-27).
If Christ lives in us then God Himself is in us; when the believer has Christ within, they will honour Him as supreme above all and walk in holiness as revealed in His word. For, *'without holiness no-one will see the Lord'* (Hebrews 12:14). Demeaning Christ, or indulging in sin, places us outside the faith.

One day our salvation will be complete. Our forgiveness was bought when we believe in Jesus, He now lives in and with us, but one day the work will be finished and we will be free from every blemish, presented *'holy, and blameless, and above reproach in His sight'* (1:22 NKJV).

Questions for Groups
Colossians 1:15-29

Please take the Bible and read the chapter out loud before answering the questions.

Who is Jesus? v15-19

1. What does an image of something enable us to do?
2. Why are we told not to make images of God in the Old Testament? Exodus 20:4-5.
3. How does Jesus make the invisible God visible? v15, v19.
4. What does the title First Born mean? v15, v18. Also, Luke 2:7, Romans 8:29, Hebrews 12:23.
5. Did you know Mary had other children? Matthew 12:46, Mark 3:31-32, Luke 8:19-21, John 2:12, Acts 1:14. What was the difference between the other children and Jesus?
6. How can we tell from this passage that Jesus is uncreated?
7. Who created the invisible thrones, dominions, principalities and powers that the false teachers were afraid of?
8. Who is Jesus?

What has He done? v20-22

1. What words here describe our natural standing before God? v21.
2. Describe the word reconciled or reconciliation?
3. Have you ever been reconciled to someone?
4. What is the cost of reconciliation? How is this cost paid by Christ?
5. Will God blame us in heaven? v22.

What is our Response? v23-29
1. What are we called to do? v23.
2. What are the two characteristics of Christians seen in v23?
3. What was Paul's response to the Gospel?
4. Why do you think Paul uses the word mystery?
5. What does he say this mystery is?
6. Knowing this, how do we make Christ pre-eminent in our lives?

To close your study, ask: Are there any practical things I need to do as a result of looking at Colossians 1?

Then pray around the issues your group has covered.

Chapter Three
THE DANGER OF DECEPTION
Colossians 2:1-23

The Danger of Deception v1-10

Look back v11-14
What God has done: (Circumcision – changed nature – changed location - forgiven.)
What we do: Baptism.

Look around v16-22
Hollow Philosophy: (Religion – experience – asceticism.)

Look up v6-7, 3:2
What we must be doing: (setting our minds – strengthening our faith – overflowing with thankfulness.)

The Church perpetually faces the problem of understanding and interpreting Christ's teaching. As ever there are two options, we can follow *'fine-sounding arguments'* (2:4), based on *'hollow and deceptive philosophy'* and *'human traditions'* (2:8) or we can come to a *'complete understanding'* of ***'the mystery of God, namely, Christ, in whom are hidden all the treasures of wisdom and knowledge'*** (2:2-3).

THE DANGER OF DECEPTION v1-10

The problem that Colosse and Laodicea are facing is one of false teaching, they are faced with *'fine sounding arguments'* (2:4), but they are based on *'hollow and deceptive philosophy'* and *'human traditions'* (2:8). They appear wise, but do not lead to God in Christ. These early Gnostics are teaching that there is a secret and mysterious knowledge that only they have. Paul, teaches that all you need is in Jesus. *'In Christ all the fullness of the Deity lives in bodily form, and you have been given fullness in Christ'* (2:9-10).

The key verses are **Colossians 2:6-7** *'just as **you received Christ** Jesus as Lord, **continue** to live in Him, **rooted** and built up in Him.'* The warning is that if their roots do not go deep into Christ, the plant will die. If our roots are not deep in God's word we will easily fall to 'deceptive philosophy.'

How are we to keep ourselves from deception?

1:   LOOK BACK AT WHAT CHRIST HAS DONE

Christianity never starts with us; it starts with what God has done. The first thing He does for the believer is cleanse them. *'In Him you were also **circumcised**, in the **putting off of the sinful nature**, not with a circumcision done by the hands of men but with the circumcision done **by Christ'*** (2:11).

i)   **What God does:** - He cuts off our sinful nature. Circumcision was the illustration of this. In the Old Covenant, the Jews were separated and holy because they were circumcised. Paul is clear that circumcision is no longer something God requires. What God requires is a *'Putting off of the sinful nature'* (2:11). We cannot follow Christ without repentance, this is basic to the Christian faith. (Mark 1:14-15, Luke 24:46-47, Acts 2:38, Hebrews 6:1.) When we come to Christ, the first thing God does is change our inward nature. We are not what we were, and cannot excuse our tendencies and temptations.

ii)   God accomplishes this by **changing our location**, we are no longer in the world, we are *'In Him'* (2:11). We need to think of this geographically as well as spiritually, our location is changed. We move from being in the world to being in Christ. The picture is twofold; we enter into Christ, just as Moses entered the cloud of Glory, but Christ also enters our living human spirits, bringing the life of the Holy Spirit. This is the new birth, our nature is changed and we are circumcised, in our inward nature. God now lives within and the old sinful nature is cut away. In its place is the New Nature, *'created to be like God in true righteousness and holiness'* (Ephesians 4:24).

God told the Israelites, *'Circumcise your hearts, therefore, and do not be stiff-necked any longer'* (Deuteronomy 10:16). If we are *'In Christ'* then God has changed our heart. *'When **you were dead** in your sins and in the uncircumcision of your sinful nature, **God made you alive with Christ. He forgave** us all our sins, having **cancelled the written code**, with its regulations, that was against us and that stood opposed to us; He took it away, nailing it to the cross'* (2:13-14).

iii)   This new life comes in two stages.
a: He gives us **Spiritual life** as we are linked to Christ, the source of life.
b: He takes the written record of our sins and nails it to the cross with Jesus (2:14).

Forgiveness costs. He doesn't just forgive our sins, He pays the price, **cancels the debt and enables us to live new lives in Christ.**

Christians use the word 'saved' but what are we saved from?

We _were_ saved from the **penalty** of sin at the cross, where Christ died as our substitute.

We _are_ saved from the **pollution** of sin at the new birth, where Christ cleanses and forgives us.

We _are_ saved from the **power** of sin, as we learn to walk in the light of His Word under the guidance of the Holy Spirit.

[It is important to realise that the Holy Spirit will never inspire any behaviour which is in contradiction to God's Holy Word. Christ the living word will always guide us in harmony with God's written word.]

We _will be_ saved from the **presence** of sin, when we step into heaven. Until then we seek to overcome temptation and if we fall, we return to the cross, the place of forgiveness. This is where the *'fullness of the Deity'* (2:9) poured out His blood for our forgiveness. The fact that God was in Christ shedding His blood on the cross, is what gives the blood its wonderful power. The blood of the cross is not just the blood of sacrifice, it is the blood of God poured out for us.

What we do: - Paul uses baptism as a symbol of our acceptance of and agreement with Christ's sacrifice. Believer's baptism is a burial and resurrection service, proclaiming that the old nature is dead and I am now living a new life 'in Christ.' Here the cleansing of the body mirrors God's cleansing of the soul. - **Baptism** is us agreeing with God that our old nature is dead and buried, and that we are raised anew *'in Christ.'* We are *'buried with him in baptism and raised with Him **through your faith** in the power of God, who raised Him from the dead'* (2:12). We are acting out what Christ has already done; believer's baptism is a sacramental cleansing of the body which mirrors God's cleansing of the soul.

Water baptism in the New Testament was not infant baptism, as we now know it, it was a burial of the old way of life, a washing away of sins and a **pledge** of the believer to follow Christ. *'Not the removal of dirt from the body but the pledge of a good conscience towards God'* (1 Peter 3:21).

In baptism, we proclaim *'We died to sin; how can we live in it any longer?'* (Romans 6:2) Baptism is the **beginning of discipleship**. It does not save the person, it proclaims they are now saved and ready to become disciples of Christ. At 'The Great Commission' Jesus clearly links it with discipleship when He says, *'Go and make disciples of all nations, baptising them in the name of the Father and of the Son and of the Holy Spirit'* (Matthew 28:18-20).

2:   LOOK AROUND AT THE DISTRACTIONS

Paul encourages us to consider the deceptions; these 'fine-sounding arguments' are 'hollow' and 'unspiritual'. They 'have the appearance of wisdom' but 'lack any value in restraining sensual indulgence,' they cannot change the heart or change our lives. This is one of our major challenges today, we argue that there is no need to change our life to become a Christian when the scripture teaches that if we remain unchanged, we remain un-Christian. However, the changes needed are not external changes, but an internal rebirth.

Three hollow philosophies are considered.   Religion - Experience - Diet.

i)   **FESTIVALS AND CEREMONIES:** *'Do not let anyone judge you... with regard to a religious festival, a New Moon celebration or a Sabbath day. These are a shadow of the things that were to come; the reality, however, is found in Christ'* (2:16-17).

Jewish rituals included Passover (April), Pentecost (May or June), the Day of Atonement (September,) the Feast of Tabernacles (Sept/October), these were commanded by God. So, why don't we celebrate them today? The answer is because they are SHADOWS, and a shadow precedes the real thing but has no substance. **Shadows bear a resemblance to, but are not, the reality itself.**

How many festivals are Christians commanded to observe? None! Christianity is supposed to be a community-based, Spirit-empowered, Word-honouring, religion-free zone!

How many ceremonies do we have? Two: Baptism and Communion. The New Testament does not give any festivals! However, we stand upon the foundation of the Old Testament, and we celebrate the reality of Redemption (Passover becomes Easter), of the coming of the Spirit (Pentecost), of cleansing (Day of Atonement – Easter) and of sojourning (Tabernacles). We need to remember the vital link between the two Testaments, they are in harmony not in disagreement. 'The New is in the Old contained, the Old is in the New explained.'

Is it wrong to celebrate Christian festivals? No, as long as the festival is not all we have, we have inherited the reality of Christ. Even the Sabbath day is not re-iterated in the New Testament. The sabbath is a gift of God, it is a principle to live by, not an enforced observance. Christians actually observe the Lord's Day, the day of resurrection and the coming of the Spirit, rather than the sabbath.

It is not wrong to celebrate Christian festivals; the problem is that it is easier to attend ceremonies and festivals than cultivate a relationship with God. Trusting in 'religion' is no good, it is empty. We must trust in Christ. We must be '*rooted and established*' in Him, not simply follow religious observance. The Jews were better at religion than anyone, Judaizers wanted to make these Colossian believers religious. God saved us from religion. Forgiveness does not come through a festival, it came through the new birth and was paid for at the cross.

What we have is a grown-up faith where you have to learn to walk with the Lord.

ii)   **EXPERIENCES:** When we take experience as our spiritual guide we are in great danger. '*Such a person goes into great detail about what he has seen, and his unspiritual mind puffs him up with idle notions. He has lost connection with the head*' (2:18-19). There are many kinds of experience; the world, the flesh and the devil can all supply counterfeit experiences (2 Corinthians 11:14). We must take our experience to The Word of God, and measure it against the unchanging canon of scripture. Experiences are subjective but The Word of God is an objective guide. If we do what the Word says should not be done, we have lost connection with the head.

In our current Church debates we are constantly encouraged to value and listen to people's experience, but experience is not always a reliable guide. We need to take great care that testimony does not supplant the Scripture. Like the false teachers in Colosse, their '*unspiritual mind puffs them up with idle notions. They have lost connection with the Head*' (2:18-19).

There are many kinds of experience, some of which are to be celebrated. Experiences can be spiritual and unspiritual. The rule is: the greater the experience, the humbler we need to be. If we value our experience, we must take it to the Word and measure it against the unchanging canon of scripture. Otherwise we will lose our connection with the head.

The specific problem for the Colossians was exalting Angelic experiences over Christ. There is a **genuine ministry of Angels**, [Billy Graham's book 'Angels', is the best I have read.]

There is a **Popular** mythology about Angels today. Any bookshop will offer titles like, 'The Angel Bible', 'Everything you wanted to know about Angels', or 'Daily guidance from your Angels'. An Angel outside Christ's authority is called a demon. We need to take care not to be deceived by our experiences. All the treasures of wisdom and knowledge are hidden in Christ (2:3).

Some things to understand about Angels.
- An Angel is an extension of the hand of God, who carries God's power. Angels have no independent thoughts or actions, they will do no more or less than God commands.
- They are not physical beings; they are spiritual beings whose desire is to minister to God's people. *'Are not all angels ministering spirits sent to serve those who will inherit salvation?'* (Hebrews 1:14)
- These people worshipped Angels, but **only God is worthy of worship**. St John Writes, *'I fell at his feet to worship Him. But He said to me, "Do not do it! I am a fellow-servant with you and with your brothers who hold to the testimony of Jesus. Worship God!"'* (Revelation 19:10) To worship Angels is a sin, as it substitutes something else for God. Every experience must lead to Christ; if they do not take us to worship at the feet of Jesus it is hollow and deceptive. Mormons claim they have another testimony of Jesus Christ revealed by an Angel, but *'see to it that no-one takes you captive through hollow and deceptive philosophy, which depends on human tradition'* (2:8-9).

- We do not chase Angels; God will send them to minister to us when they are needed, but they are at God's command and all we need of God is found in Jesus.

iii) **DIET AND ASCETICISIM:** *'You died with Christ to the basic principles of this world, why, as though you still belonged to it, do you submit to its rules: "Do not handle! Do not taste! Do not touch!"?'* (2:20-22). These are based on human commands and teachings. Here, we are looking at fasting and food laws. This is **Religion by Rules**, there is a danger for the Church.

Jesus is clear on this; ceremonial food was never a means to knowing God (Matthew 15:17-20). The Old Testament food laws were mainly for the health of God's people not about getting close to God. The Jewish food laws were abolished for Christians at the Council of Jerusalem, and few restrictions were placed on believers. *'It seemed good to the Holy Spirit and to us to lay upon you no greater burden than these necessary things: that you abstain from things offered to idols, from blood, from things strangled, and from sexual immorality. If you keep yourselves from these, you will do well'* (Acts 15:28-29). The Jewish dietary laws were never applied to the church. Food and drink are not a moral issue but a human preference, like 'which day to worship', 'what to wear' or 'which hymn book to use'. The question is "Do we love Jesus?" If so, lead a life of 'Scriptural Holiness' and avoid sexual immorality.

I have heard it argued that we are free to reinterpret God's moral laws on sexual behaviour because they are the equivalent of the food laws and no longer apply to Christians. This is not so. God's moral commands stand, we are to abstain 'from sexual immorality.' The danger is that we can make our own Christian rules, and then keep them and think we are doing well. Then we look down on those who do not keep our set of rules. These can be rules about how we dress, about how to worship, rules about buildings, teetotalism verses, moderate drinking and Sundays.

Don't fall out about these. For a generation, they became the mark of Christianity. The question is, do we walk in the light of God's word? Are we repentant of our sins? Are we a new creation in Christ? Some things are optional, but sexual immorality is not optional. God's Word is clear, the gift of a sexual relationship is given to a man and a woman who are married. Sex is the sign of their covenant relationship (Matthew 19:4-6).

What about fasting? Fasting is part of the Christian faith. John the Baptist's disciples asked Jesus why His followers were not fasting, *'Jesus answered, "How can the guests of the bridegroom mourn while he is with them? The time will come when the bridegroom will be taken from them; then they will fast"'* (Matthew 9:15). True fasting is done in secret, it is a season where people abstain from food to pray and seek God. Jesus said, *"when you fast, put oil on your head and wash your face, so that it will not be obvious to others that you are fasting, but only to your Father, who is unseen; and your Father, who sees what is done in secret, will reward you"* (Matthew 6:17-18).

A fast is a time to withdraw from the world and dedicate ourselves to seeking God in Spirit, Soul and Body. It is not a religious ordinance but an opportunity to interact with God our Father, through the blood of Christ, in the power of the Holy Spirit.

Religion by rules has a problem, it does not work, it may seem disciplined but it cannot change the heart. *'Such regulations indeed have an appearance of wisdom, with their self-imposed worship, their false humility and their harsh treatment of the body, but they lack any value in restraining sensual indulgence'* (2:23).

3:   LOOK UP TO CHRIST

Lastly Paul says that, to avoid deception, we must look up: He says this even more clearly in Colossians 3:2 *'Set your minds on things above, not on earthly things.'* We need a mindset that plays the narrative of heaven and not mere human wisdom.

What should we do? *'Just as you received Christ Jesus as Lord, continue to live in Him, rooted and built up in Him, strengthened in the faith as you were taught, and overflowing with thankfulness'* (2:6-7).

i)   We need to strengthen our faith in Him. Early Christians were committed to, *'the apostles' doctrine and fellowship'* (Acts 2:42). This is where we are rooted; we strengthen our faith in the teaching and fellowship of the local church. To be rooted in Christ, Sunday alone is not enough, hearing sermons is not enough, we must seek to know for ourselves the great mysteries of God in Christ. Christianity is not a hobby, it is a life-style of Scriptural Holiness. If we are in doubt, deception always seeks to re-define the word of God by asking, *'Did God really say?'* (Genesis 3:1)

ii)   *'And overflowing with thankfulness'* (2:7). Grumbling, moaning and thanklessness will stop our faith dead. There is a lot to moan about, but it creates a negative outlook, it is poison to the soul and splits apart people who love the Lord. A person of faith majors on thankfulness. Are you thankful for the ones you love? Do they know it? Are you thankful for your brothers and sisters in Christ? Have you told any of them? Ask yourself, am I a thankful person and who should I thank this week?

At home I recommend using TCP. To show someone you are thankful takes Time, Compliments and Presents.

Someone may ask what they have to be thankful for. If you have put your faith in Christ, you are alive from the dead, your sins are washed and nailed to the cross, your old life is buried and you are living in the power of the resurrection. You are freed from empty rules and brought in to the Mystery of God in Christ. You are rooted in the soil of heaven and you will live for eternity. All God asks is that you continue as you started. Follow Christ, and when you fall be cleansed again by the blood of the cross.

Questions for Groups
Colossians 2:1-23

Please take the Bible and read the chapter out loud before answering the questions.

1. Where does a Christian go for wisdom and knowledge? v2-3.
2. Chapter two continues to describe the supremacy of Jesus. How is He introduced in this chapter? v2, 3, 9.
3. What is Paul's chief concern in this passage? v6-7.
4. What can cause believers to stop growing spiritually and lose their vitality?
5. Why does Paul mention baptism? v12.
6. What does it mean to be circumcised by Christ? v11.
7. What three things does Christ do for us? v13-14.
8. How does the law stand against us? v14.
9. What was nailed to the cross? v14.
10. What was made a public spectacle on the cross? v15.
11. How is the false teaching described? v4, 8, 20, 22.
12. What are the three areas of hollow and deceptive philosophy Paul gives us a warning against? v16-18, 22.
13. Do people follow these today?
14. Do they work? v23.
15. What do verses 6 and 7 instruct us to do?

To close your study, ask: Are there any practical things I need to do as a result of looking at Colossians 2?

Then pray around the issues your group has covered.

Chapter Four
DEVELOPING SPIRITUAL FRUIT
Colossians 3:1-17

Keys to Spiritual Growth

Putting Off v1-9, 12-13
(You died – a spiritual change - inward sins – spoken sins.)

Putting On v10-15
(Restoration of attitudes, forgiveness and love.)

Guiding Lights v16-17
(The peace of God – The Word of God - the heart of Praise.)

Paul gives us 2 key actions in overcoming temptation and developing spiritual fruit: 1: Putting off. 2: Putting on.

1:   PUTTING OFF

When you placed your Faith in Christ the 'old you' died. *'For you died, and your life is hidden with Christ in God'* (3:3). *'Put to death, therefore, whatever belongs to your earthly nature: sexual immorality, impurity, lust, evil desires and greed, which is idolatry'* (3:5).

The picture of the Christian we are given is of a living Spirit and a dead body. *'But if Christ is in you, your body is dead because of sin, yet your spirit is alive because of righteousness'* (Romans 8:10). Baptism actually enacts this death and burial.

The part that connects Spirit and the body is the **soul**. (Mind, Emotions & Will.)

The question here is **where is your mind set?** Is it set on Christ or set in this world? *'Seek those things which are above... Set your mind on things above, not on things on the earth'* (3:1-2). What fills your heart and mind will profoundly affect your life. Are you preoccupied with worry- Plans – Books – TV - the News? The choice is yours; you must learn to set your mind on things above and draw strength from God's very presence.

We are told to put off our old attitudes; God does not do it for us, we must *'put off all these'* (3:8). This is **not** just about our **will power**; it is about **which kingdom** we draw strength from. A profound change takes place when someone comes to faith in Christ.

We change our spiritual condition. We are brought from death to life, *'you were dead in your sins but God made you alive with Christ'* (2:13).

We change our kingdom. As we move from darkness to light, we become *'partakers of the inheritance of the saints in the light... He has delivered us from the power of darkness and brought us into the kingdom of the Son He loves'* (1:12-13).

We change our standing. We were enemies, now we are reconciled. *'Once you were alienated from God and were enemies in your minds because of your evil behaviour. But now He has reconciled you'* (1:21-22).

God comes to live within us. *'For in Christ all the fullness of the Deity lives in bodily form, and you have been given fullness in Christ'* (2:9-10).

Because we are changed people, there are things we are to put off.

Paul separates these into two categories.

i)   **Sins of the heart** *'sexual immorality, impurity, lust, evil desires and greed, which is idolatry'* (3:5).
Jesus understood that the inward life affects our outward actions. *"Out of the heart come evil thoughts, murder, adultery, sexual immorality, theft, false testimony, slander. These are what make you 'unclean'"* (Matthew 15:18-20). No one else can see these, but God does and the attitude of our heart will eventually show. Through confession and repentance, we need to put off these inward temptations.

ii)   **Our words.** People cannot see our hearts but they can hear our words. *'You yourselves are to put off all these: anger, wrath, malice, blasphemy, filthy language out of your mouth. Do not lie to one another'* (3:8-9 NKJV).

We probably sin in our words more than any other area. Do you ever suffer from foot in mouth disease? It comes from the old self not from Christ; there is no excuse for addressing a brother or sister in Christ with *'anger, rage, malice, slander and filthy language or lies.'* James puts it clearly *'The tongue also is a fire, a world of evil among the parts of the body. It corrupts the whole person, sets the whole course of his life on fire and is itself set on fire by hell'* (James 3:6). Our words betray our hearts, better say nothing than wound a brother or sister in Christ. We are to put these things off like old worn out clothes.

2:   WHAT ARE WE TO PUT ON?

*'Put on the new self, which is **being renewed** in **knowledge**, in the image of its Creator'* (3:10). The **process** is not finished yet. When God took us on, He took **on a restoration project. He is restoring the lost** 'image of God' (see Gen 1:26-27). This only comes from the presence of the Holy Spirit.

The test comes in how we treat each other. *'Therefore, as God's chosen people, holy and dearly loved, clothe yourselves with compassion, kindness, humility, gentleness and patience. Bear with each other and forgive* **whatever grievances** *you may have against one another. Forgive as the Lord forgave you'* (3:12-13).

There is a difference between patience and long- suffering. Patience is usually shown when facing intractable and difficult circumstances, whereas long- suffering is usually shown in the interaction with difficult people. Few of us exhibit both of these qualities, we will always have grievances, and difficulties, but we are forgiven and are called to forgive.

We need an attitude adjustment; we are to put on **new attitudes like new clothes**, *'clothe yourselves'* [we have to clothe ourselves, God will not do it]. These attitudes give us a picture of the Lord Jesus and He expects these attitudes to live in us. You may say 'but I don't feel like putting them on'. The answer is to, well, put them on and they will affect your feelings.

Feelings follow decisions. If you decide to act in a loving way, you will begin to love; if you act in a forgiving way, you will begin to forgive. Do not let your fleshly feelings dominate your spiritual life. *'Set your mind on things above, not on things on the earth'* (3:2). Where do you draw your energy from?

Grievances test our character. I have met people whose grievances consume them, it is all they can think about. I remember Jean telling me what she believed happened after the death of her mother. She suspected that her mother kept her money in the brass railing above the fireplace. When she arrived at the house, her sister had already removed the railing and told Jean, "it was empty." From that day forward, there was no trust or love between these two sisters. It became a persistent, unforgiven grievance. Jean had been healed of painful leg ulcers at our church in answer to prayer, but never came to full faith in Christ. Unforgiveness was one of the contributing factors.

'*And* over all these virtues put on love, which binds them all together in perfect unity' (3:14). Love is described here as a belt making the clothes fit. If our doctrine does not lead us to love God's people, we have got our doctrine wrong. For '*love will cover a multitude of sins*' (1 Peter 4:8). Good doctrine leads to loving actions.

The greatest commandment is not to understand God but to love God; I don't always understand my wife, but I do love her. [John Haggy says "God never commanded a man to understand his wife; He commanded him to love her."] Our understanding and our knowledge are still being renewed. We will never understand all things, but we can love as Christ loved. How is your attitude? Are you wearing the attitude of Christ? The sign that we are living in love is thankfulness '*and always be thankful*' (3:15 TLB). Our aim should be to be thankful rather than critical.

We do need to take one word of caution, love is not an excuse for ignoring sin. There is a new gospel being preached in our churches, a message that links inclusiveness and love, but ignores repentance and the new birth. We are not saved by the love of God, we are saved by faith in the blood of Christ. Paul is calling the Colossians to love one another, but to stand firmly against any gospel that does not insist on the fruit of holiness. Repentance and faith are still the doorway into the kingdom of God (Mark 1:15). A renewed life that turns from sin is still the sign that the Spirit of Christ is at work within any individual. The message is always one of invitation to all, but on the day of judgement, only those who have come in repentance and faith will be included. The gospel of inclusiveness is a popular, dangerous and counterfeit gospel. It is one step from universalism, the false belief that all will finally be saved.

3:   THREE GUIDING LIGHTS

In our walk with Jesus, God has given us three guides to accompany us.

i)   **The peace of Christ:** *'Let the peace of Christ **rule** in your hearts'* (3:15). The word for rule is 'referee' or if you are a cricket fan, 'umpire'. The Holy Spirit has three distinct ministries **Convicting, Comforting and Empowering,** the Holy Spirit never brings condemnation. *'There is therefore now no condemnation for those who are in Christ Jesus'* (Romans 8:1). If we feel condemned, then that is not the work of the Holy Spirit.

The Holy Spirit will unsettle our peace when we sin.

The moment we lose our sense of peace and detect conviction, the Holy Spirit is calling us to confession. Repentance is an ongoing process. We do not simply repent when we are converted, we need to learn to repent of each action and attitude that offends the Holy Spirit of God. He will bring to mind that thing that has caused His peace to leave and until we confess and put things right, we will not find His peace restored. When the referee blows the whistle it means we have broken the rules of the game and so the game stops. When we lose our peace, we must stop and put right the offence before continuing to walk with Christ. The presence of peace or the absence of peace is our guide, *'the peace of Christ is to rule in our hearts'* (3:15). When we sense a lack of peace and a growing turmoil within, we need to listen to the ruling Holy

Spirit, since it is His ministry to bring the settled peace of God into our hearts and lives. God's peace is given as our guide; the lack of peace is a warning that all is not well and we need to return to God in humility, confessing our sin, remembering that 'Christ did not die for our excuses, Christ died for our sins.'

The problem is that some people have walked so long without putting things right that they have pushed the Holy Spirit away and forgotten what the peace of God feels like. The Holy Spirit came to convict us of sin, not to condemn us. Once we have sought cleansing, His peace returns and we continue with a testimony of forgiveness, walking in the peace of God, loving God and loving people.

He will also bring conviction if we are planning to go the wrong way. We should learn to listen to the prompting of the Holy Spirit. Sometimes the Holy Spirit convicts us as we contemplate sin. The moment we are tempted, the Holy Spirit unsettles our peace. If the flesh prompts us to follow after *'sexual immorality, impurity, lust, evil desires and greed, anger, rage, malice, slander and filthy language'* (3:5), we need to confess the temptation and repent. When we entertain these thoughts, it is wearing our 'old clothes.' The peace of God is supposed to rule our hearts, rather than the passions of the flesh.

ii)   **The guidance of the Word**: *'Let the word of Christ dwell in you richly'* (Col 3:16). God's Word cannot dwell in us if we don't know it. How many ways do you know of reading the Bible? We can study, search, meditate upon and memorise the Bible. A business man worked out how many pages his Bible had and divided the number by 365, the answer came out as 3.5. He then read 3 ½ pages a day before work in order to read through the Bible in a year. We can study, in groups or on our own. The question is, does God's word dwell in us richly? It is there to guide our thoughts and actions. Our guide for moral decisions is not the changing attitudes of society, but the unchanging word of God. We are to use God's word as our guide.

The word speaks into our situation, the Bible makes a distinction between the 'Logos' the eternal word, and the 'Rhema' a specific or 'now' word. The preached and the prophetic word can speak directly to our situation so that the eternal word becomes the now word for us. Most importantly, God will never inspire us to do something that His Word specifically condemns. The word and the Spirit are one, in their guidance all guidance leads to holiness. If we find ourselves in clear violation of God's will revealed in His word, we cannot reason our way round it, rather we must come in repentance and humility. God's word is *still 'a lamp to your path and a light to your feet'* (Psalm 119:105). Rationalising away our sinful behaviour will not bring us back into the peace of God. The rule is simple in matters of morality, the Word is inspired and reason is fallible, as Doctor Martyn Luther discovered, reason must be captive to the word of God. This is an unchanging principle of guidance.

iii)   **The heart fixed on praise:** Praise has a strong link with thankfulness. *'Sing psalms, hymns and spiritual songs with gratitude in your hearts to God'* (3:16).

Praise focuses our spirit on God and changes our attitude. There has been a rediscovery of the power of praise over the last 30 years. People have come to see praise and worship as the means of entry into God's presence. *'Enter his gates with thanksgiving and his courts with praise'* (Psalm 100:4). Those who enter through the gates of praise find the presence of God. Praise is more than singing a song on Sunday, it is entering whole-heartedly into the joy of the Lord, through the expression of a song.

Discouragement stops praise and sin stops praise, however forgiveness releases praise. How many of our hymns have this testimony, 'my chains fell off, my heart was free?' Forgiveness brings forth a testimony of praise. When our mind is set on things above we will be filled with praise. We may not always feel like praising, but as we give ourselves to praising our wonderful Saviour our feelings will follow. This is an instruction to be obeyed, rather than a suggestion to be considered. *'Sing psalms, hymns and spiritual songs with gratitude in your hearts to God'* (3:16).

Paul uses varied means of praise as he offers psalms, perhaps he knew the tunes? Since we do not, we can always offer a Psalm to our own tunes. He offered hymns, which has been the practice of the church throughout the ages. He also offered songs inspired by the Spirit, 'spiritual songs,' perhaps spontaneous? As he did this it was not the head that was engaged, but the heart. His songs were the expression of a grateful heart, and so must ours be.

If we are to be fruitful, we must learn to put off the old self with its attitudes and words that wound. We must fix our minds on Christ and put on the new self, with a changed attitude. We must learn to listen to the guiding peace of the Holy Spirit and dwell richly in Christ's word until it dwells richly in us. We must forgive as Christ forgave, continually lifting our hearts in praise. As we do, we will be setting our minds on things above and we will begin to be renewed inside. Our inward attitudes and outward expressions will soon become attitudes that please God Himself.

Questions for groups
Colossians 3:1-17

Please take the Bible and read the chapter out loud before answering the questions.

1. Where is the mind of a Christian set? v1-2. How might we do this?
2. In verse 5 and verse 8 we are given two instructions, what are they?
3. Can you identify the sins of the heart mentioned here? Are these common? What is God's assessment of them? v6.
4. What are the sins of the lips mentioned here? v8-9. Why are these serious?
5. What image is God seeking to restore in us? v10.
6. What are we to put on? v12, v14. What does this mean? Does God do this or do we?
7. Why must we forgive others? v13.
8. What is the place of repentance in the gospel message?
9. What three things help us in our Christian walk? v15-16. Explain these.
10. How has your life changed since you came to faith in Christ?
11. Spend a few moments thanking Jesus for forgiveness as you pray together.

To close your study, ask: Are there any practical things I need to do as a result of looking at Colossians 3?

Then pray around the issues your group has covered.

Chapter Five
THE POWER OF THE GOSPEL
Colossians 4:1-18

1: The Gospel and the power of prayer v2-7, 12
(Consistent, Watchful, Specific, Focused, Earnest and Thankful.)

2: The Privilege of witnessing v5-6
(Opportunity - Clarity.)

3: The Presence of Friends v7-18
(Team ministry – Service and Forgiveness.)

There are no 'Lone Ranger' Christians - even the Lone Ranger had Tonto. To be effective we need a passionate prayer life, a heart that is ready to witness and a team around us.

Epaphras has come to Paul seeking his wisdom about the false teaching he is facing. The Colossians and Epaphras needed Paul. Now Paul calls on them for prayer, Paul needs them. He is in prison in Rome and his teaching on prayer is very instructive.

1:   THE GOSPEL AND THE POWER OF PRAYER v2-7, 12

What are we doing when we pray? Is prayer an attempt to persuade God that He should fall into line with our will and desires? Is it insisting on God doing things 'my way?' No, it is praying 'your will be done' and bringing our lives in line with God's best will for us. If we do not pray, there are things on earth that will not be accomplished as God intends them to be. Prayer is placing our will into agreement with the will of God, so that His purposes may be accomplished through and in us.

How do we know what God wants? He will never ordain anything on earth that is in clear violation of His written word. His aim is not always to change our circumstances, but to use us where we are and work in us in whatever circumstances we find ourselves.

How should we pray? We are to be consistent, watchful, specific, focused, earnest and thankful in prayer. *'Devote yourselves to prayer'* (4:2). We never finish learning how to pray. When did you last read a book on prayer that encouraged and enabled you to go deeper with God? Prayer is not an occasional thing, for the Christian it is the very breath of life. We need to be consistent in prayer; this is probably the highest calling of each day, to spend time in the presence of our Heavenly Father.

To be 'Watchful' is to be alert to the situations and circumstances around us. We need to see what needs to be brought before God in prayer, in our family, in the church, in the news and in the nation. *'I urge, then, first of all, that requests, prayers, intercession and thanksgiving be made for everyone-- for kings and all those in authority, that we may live peaceful and quiet lives in all godliness and holiness'* (1Timothy 2:1-2).

Prayer is to be wide ranging in its scope but **specific in its requests**. Paul asks for a specific need. A very bad prayer is the one commonly prayed from the book of prayer, 'we pray for all people everywhere according to their need.' A prayer should be specific enough to know you have been answered.

Prayer is hard work *'Epaphras ... is always **wrestling** in prayer for you, that you may stand firm in all the will of God, mature and fully assured'* (4:12). Wrestling is also translated **striving** ASV, **labouring earnestly** NAS, **labouring fervently** KJV,

remembering you earnestly RSV. Prayer is hard work, it requires earnest dedication and the carving out of time to do it well.

There will come times when we do not know how to pray, but the Holy Spirit leads and intercedes, this was Paul's experience. *'In the same way, the Spirit helps us in our weakness. We do not know what we ought to pray for, but the Spirit Himself intercedes for us with groans that words cannot express.'* (Romans 8:26). This is a fervency in prayer that is available to all, and if we do not know how to pray in English, we can ask God to give us a language of prayer so that we can pray in tongues.

The word we use for earnest prayer is 'intercession,' standing between God and the need, fervently labouring and earnestly wrestling until we have an answer from God on the other person's behalf. The reason we are able to intercede is because Christ is our intercessor, who stands between God and ourselves, showing His wounds and pleading our case.

If prayer is hard work it is also a joy; as we pour out our prayers He pours in His joy. We are to be watchful and **thankful.**

Remember there are three possible answers to a prayer - Yes, No, and Wait, each can be God's will for our lives and we must be ready for His answers not our insistence. I am sure Jacob did not want pain in his hip, and a persistent limp. But it was after he met with God that his life was changed and he became Israel. Meeting God changed his spiritual life and his physical life. When he could no longer rely on his own strength, he had to rely on God. Do we pray so little because we think we can do it ourselves?

Epaphras not only sought out the advice of the Apostle, but he wrestled with God for his church. If you want your church to grow and to stand, prayer is essential. Prayer will either lead to intervention or opportunity, there is a clear link with the spread of the Gospel and our prayer life. The old but true saying is P.U.S.H.-- Pray Until Something Happens!

2:   THE PRIVILEGE OF WITNESSING v5-6

We need to remember that Paul is writing from prison (4:3) and he prays for an **open door,** but not the one we would expect. He specifically asks that **God will open a door for the Message,** not of the prison. Even in prison his concern is the spread of the Gospel. We might think there were no opportunities in prison but we would be wrong. Later in 2 Timothy Paul does ask for prayers for his release, but his first desire is the spread of the Gospel.

These prayers were answered. When he later writes to the Philippians, he has seen a fruitful ministry in the prison. *'Now I want you to know, brothers and sisters, that what has happened to me has really served to advance the gospel. As a result, it has become clear throughout the whole palace guard and to everyone else that I am in chains for Christ'* (Philippians 1:12-13).   His closing greeting also shows that the message has spread to the highest corridors of power. *'All the saints send you greetings, especially those who belong to Caesar's household'* (Philippians 4:22).

That means that if we don't have any opportunities to witness, then either God has not opened the door or we are not praying for an open door. Remember we are not looking for the doors we open but the doors God opens. Because of His great love for people, opportunities are all around us.

Rick Warren describes moving with God as surfing the waves of the sea. We do not make the wave, we look expectantly for the wave He is sending. Wesley was more proactive. People told him not to be so forceful in witness, but wait until someone asked him to share his faith. He found himself travelling in a carriage and so waited for the opportunity to say something to arise. When it did not come after an hour, he decided to take the opportunity and share his faith anyway! If we are prayerful there are always opportunities to share our faith with others.

Paul seeks to **proclaim the Gospel clearly**, but understands that how we speak is important. *'Be wise in the way you act towards outsiders; make the most of every opportunity. Let your conversation be always full of grace, seasoned with salt, so that you may know how to answer everyone'* (4:5-6).

The way we act and react is watched. Are we honest in business? Is our speech clean and encouraging? Is our conduct moral? It is no use praying like heaven and living like hell. The first rule of witnessing is - do not cause offence. Our manner and our attitude to people outside the Church is very important. Do they feel they are loved? Are you someone who values them as God values them? They are not just people to witness to but people who are deeply loved and important to God. It has been said that 'people do not care how much you know, until they know how much you care.' It is not the whole truth, but carries a warning about our attitude. Each time we share our faith, we need to speak with love and truth, genuinely caring for the person we encounter.

We are to live Godly lives and *'Make the most of every opportunity'*.

As we seek to share our faith in Christ we should ask who we can show God's kindness to at home, as we travel, in our street, when we are out shopping, in our work and in our leisure. God has appointments for us to keep; we need to *'Pray that we may **proclaim the gospel clearly**, as we should'* (4:4) and understand that we are *'created in Christ Jesus to do good works, which God prepared in advance for us to do'* (Ephesians 2:10).

We are to share in the gentlest and wisest way we can. *'Let your conversation be always full of grace, seasoned with salt, so that you may know how to answer everyone'* (4:6).

The challenge comes when we meet someone we profoundly disagree with. If we meet someone consulting a clairvoyant, how would we engage in conversation? Perhaps it is good to ask why? To explore their sense of loss? To ask, do you think it is wise? To explain where the power really comes from? Either they are a charlatan, deceiving people or else they are in touch with evil spirits, since the scripture is clear, *'man is destined to die once, and after that to face judgement'* (Hebrews 9:27).

What if someone says the Bible is all old myths and fables and can't be trusted? Do we get angry or do we ask which part they mean? When did you last read it? Have you read the life of Jesus recently?

Someone once said to me that the Scriptures were written years after by people who made up the stories, so they thought we could not possibly trust them. I took them to the introduction to Luke's Gospel, *'Many have undertaken to draw up an account of the things that have been fulfilled among us, just as they were handed down to us by those who from the first were **eye-witnesses** and servants of the word. Therefore, since I myself have **carefully investigated** everything from* the beginning, it seemed good also to me to write an **orderly account** for you, most excellent Theophilus, so that you may **know the certainty** of the things you have been taught' (Luke 1:1-4). Later I posted them a Luke's gospel and asked them to read it. The next time we met they said, "Now I have a whole different set of questions." They had moved from disbelief to investigation.

It may help to point out that many famous people have found help from the Bible - John Wayne, Errol Flynn, Napoleon, Isaac Newton, William Gladstone, Florence Nightingale, Elvis Presley, Glenn Hoddle, Kriss Akabusi to name a few - and we can also say 'I do too'. Perhaps you could find wisdom and strength if you began to read the Bible. Opportunity is all around us, we need to be ready to make the most of every one that arises.

3:   THE PRESENCE OF FRIENDS v7-18

Paul closed his letter by introducing us to his team (4:7-17). Throughout Paul's letters we see that he did not work alone; **he had a team** that shared in God's mission and ministry with him. If we are to grow as a church, it will be a team effort. Christianity is a team sport, and in Paul's team, we have Epaphras, Tychicus, Onesimus, Aristarchus, Mark, Luke and Demas - and they all have a story.

Tychicus is highly commended by Paul, '*a dear brother, a faithful minister and fellow-servant in the Lord*' (4:7). He carried Paul's letter to Colosse. If he had failed there would be no book of Colossians. He also carried Paul's personal news and greetings to the church (4:9). He was accompanied by Onesimus.

Onesimus is famous as the runaway slave belonging to Philemon. He sought to escape his Christian master, and fled to Rome, but he could not escape God. His name means useful and Paul makes a play on words, '*I appeal to you for my son Onesimus, who became my son while I was in chains. Formerly he was useless to you, but now he has become useful both to you and to me. I am sending him - who is my very heart - back to you. I would have liked to keep him with me so that he could take your place in helping me while I am in chains for the gospel. But I did not want to do anything without your consent, so that any favour you do will be spontaneous and not forced. Perhaps the reason he was separated from you for a little while was that you might have him back for good - no longer as a slave, but better than a slave, as a dear brother*' (Philemon 10-15).

Is this why Paul writes; '*Masters, provide your slaves with what is right and fair, because you know that you also have a Master in heaven*' (4:1)?

Christianity was the great leveller. It lifted slaves to the status of sons and brothers in Christ. Onesimus was forgiven by God, but he still had to show his faith by repentance and face his sins against Philemon. Paul is his advocate, seeking reconciliation and forgiveness.

Mark & Luke are here as well, two of the gospel writers are standing with Paul in prison at Rome. We know that Luke travelled with Paul often. He was Greek by birth and a doctor by profession (4:10, 14). Greeks were educated and skilful physicians; they were the first to trace the circulation of the blood through the body.

Luke does not just write the book of Acts, but witnesses the book of Acts. He first appears in Acts 16 travelling to Philippi with Paul, where Lydia is converted. Luke stays in Philippi with the infant church, when Paul moves on. Then, when Paul returns in Acts 20:6, Luke sails for Jerusalem, stopping at Troas where Eutychus dies as he falls from the third-floor window and is raised from the dead in answer to Paul's prayers. He later stays in the house of Philip the evangelist and with Mnason on the way to Jerusalem. *'Some of the disciples from Caesarea accompanied us and brought us to the home of Mnason where we were to stay. He was a man from Cyprus and one of the early disciples. When we arrived at Jerusalem, the brothers received us warmly'* (Acts 21:16-17). The repetition of the word 'us' and 'we' shows Luke's presence.

Luke accompanies Paul on the trip to Rome and suffers the ship-wreck on Malta; so, when Paul arrives in Rome Luke is with him. Luke has an able mind, collecting the early history of the life of Jesus from the eye witnesses and setting it down for us. He then chronicles the growth of the early church.

What About Mark, Paul's comment on him is a strange sentence. *'Aristarchus sends you his greetings, as does Mark, the cousin of Barnabas. (You have received instructions about him; if he comes to you, welcome him'* (4:10).

Mark's history is chequered. He went with Barnabas and Saul on their first journey to Cyprus, but halfway through returned to Jerusalem. When Barnabas wanted to take him on the second journey Paul strongly disagreed and they parted company. There is no record of Paul and Barnabas ever working together again, but it seems Barnabas's generous spirit was the right one. Mark had a ministry after all. Here Paul tells the Church not to discriminate against Mark, but to welcome him, obviously his previous problems were known but now he had proven himself and stood alongside Paul when he was imprisoned at Rome. In his last letter to Timothy, Paul specifically requests Mark's help, he tells Timothy to *'Get Mark and bring him with you, because he is helpful to me in my ministry'* (2 Timothy 4:11).

Mark is an example of someone who was slow to grow, who needed encouragement, but became a great blessing to the Church. He got a second chance and later became the author of Mark's Gospel. St Papias (c 130AD) tells us that Mark became 'the interpreter of Peter' who wrote 'accurately, howbeit not in order' 'all that was said and done by the Lord.' 'He kept a single aim in view: not to omit anything of what he heard, not to state anything therein falsely.'

Paul worked with a team of people who each contributed their gifts. Paul's team were devoted to prayer and ready to make the most of every opportunity. Each was different, but each combined to make Paul's mission the success it was. If our churches are to grow again, it will take each one of us combining in prayer and witness, using our own gifts to make it happen.

Here Paul closes, knowing a successful mission under God will take one more thing, it will take God's **grace.** To be able to stand against deception and the fine sounding arguments of people, and see the church established on truth, we will always need the grace of God. *'Grace be with you'* (4:18). Amen.

Questions for Groups
Colossians 4:1-18

Please take the Bible and read the chapter out loud before answering the questions.

1. What are the characteristics of prayer in v2-3?
2. What specific prayer does Paul ask?
3. How did Epaphras pray? v12
4. What helps you to pray?
5. How should we act towards those outside the church?
6. In v5, what does 'redeem the time' mean? What do other Bible versions say?
7. What does speech that is 'with grace and seasoned with salt' sound like?
8. What do we know about Tychicus?
9. Who was Onesimus? Look at Philemon, for an answer (see Philemon v1). To Philemon he was a slave, who was he to Paul?
10. Think of a friend who helped you come to faith, and describe their character in a sentence or two.
11. How many people are with Paul in Rome?
12. Why is Paul cautious about Mark? v10, Acts 12:12 + 25, Acts 15:37-39, 2 Timothy 4v11.
13. Who has encouraged your faith?
14. Who can you encourage this week?
15. How do we receive grace? 1:6, Hebrews 4:16, Titus 2:11.

To close your study: ask yourself 'Are there any practical things I need to do as a result of looking at Colossians 4?'

What are the key lessons each member of the group has learned over these five sessions? (There may be several.)

Pray together around the issues your group has covered.